the words of a madman.
by caitlin kelly

the words of a madman   caitlin kelly

for the broken and healing.

the words of a madman   caitlin kelly

!

warning:
this book addresses a lot of
controversial subjects, and touchy
topics.

so to the close minded people:
there's your warning.

!

table of contents:

author's note

.... 4

chapter 1: folie

.... 6

chapter 2: noyade

.... 23

chapter 3: perdu

.... 56

chapter 4: cassé

.... 75

chapter 5: coeur brisé

.... 94

chapter 6: amour

.... 136

chapter 7: finalement

.... 175

the words of a madman   caitlin kelly

author's note.

hello fellow reader. this is poetry, somewhat. written by a mentally unstable teenager, somewhat. please keep in mind, this is all completely personal. there are poems that don't specifically relate to me, however, and are written for the reader's enjoyment. specific things i would like to warn you about are, yes, this book faces mental illness, including depression and anxiety. yes, those are common world issues, yes, we need more awareness cause there are young teenagers locking themselves in their rooms, crying themselves to sleep at night, wanting to die. sorry for being graphic, but hey it's true. this world isn't this lovely cloud where we can frolic in the fields of dandelions and sunshine. the world is fucking cruel and we're humans so we can't always handle it. we have our ups and downs and we have people to rely on and trust and we have people that break our trust. this book, is

the words of a madman					caitlin kelly

about. being real. being broken. being happy. being sad. being anxious. being in love. being depressed. and, overall, being human.

to all the young readers, we have a voice, we can change things, stand up for what you believe in, and we can make this world a better place for equality, for the LGBTQ community, for the women and for everything else that this world needs to stand for. we're all the same under all that skin to the bone, so let's act like it. if you are ever feeling depressed or suicidal please call this number: 1-800-273-8255. now, let's jump right into the words written by a madman.

chapter 1.
folie.
madness

the words of a madman caitlin kelly

flow.
10/05/2017

they say poetry is for
the broken
because it's so well
spoken

all the poems i write
are ideas at night

the poetry about you
could be its own
tune

because it flows so
well.

drained.

    I never planned on being depressed. It never really phased me. but a year after all the bullying and pain. just seeing everyone move on with life just killed my insides. i felt so phased in the past. i just hurt seeing their faces.

the words of a madman   caitlin kelly

10:54 pm
the monster under the bed
has become the monster inside my head

the words of a madman   caitlin kelly

yes i'm here
except there's something
new about me

i have this cloud you see

it just kind of hovers over my head

and rains on me whenever it wants

yeah it's kind of annoying

and yeah people think it's made up for attention

only the true ones will stay until they can see it

and when they can
some will walk away
cause they don't want to be in it's path of
rain

    - *my depression cloud*

the words of a madman   caitlin kelly

it's so funny
how poetry
can make
anything
sound
beautiful and
human
poetry just
lets you know
that being
human is
normal
and feeling
pain
is beautiful

alright okay fine

**i'm fine
i'm fine
i'm fine**

**it's okay
it's okay
it's okay**

**i'm alright
i'm alright
i'm alright**

the words of a madman   caitlin kelly

intentions are different
than
predictions

the words of a madman   caitlin kelly

you know you've
lost your will
to live when
you don't walk on the
sidewalk anymore
and you don't
look before crossing
the road

the words of a madman　　　　　caitlin kelly

my heart is beating
yet i don't feel alive
i feel like i'm trapped in a dream
screaming to get out
yet watching myself live my life
like i'm on autopilot
but i can't find the off button

    -   *depersonalization*

the words of a madman   caitlin kelly

they'll never hear you scream
how much you hate yourself
at night
and that will kill you
but you'll also be
relieved
that they don't have to see
you go through that
pain.

the words of a madman   caitlin kelly

chapter no one
wants to see.

there's that gray area
no one will talk about
there's that chapter
that no one will read
there's the broken pieces
no one will pick up and
claim the reasons for them
people don't want to talk
about the pain and that's what
makes it so hurtful to others
since they don't have anyone
to talk to
or anyone that relates to them
the broken pieces don't just vanish after time

the words of a madman   caitlin kelly

i talk about my depression like it's a whole
other person
you see
it is
it's not me
well it's a part of me
but people classify me
as my depression
which isn't true
because i wouldn't
choose to tell myself
to die
or that my
worth isn't
alive
my depression is
just kinda of
there…
    -   it's not me i swear

the words of a madman   caitlin kelly

you said you would help me
but all you did was
hand me the knife
and tell me
to be happy

- suicide

the words of a madman   caitlin kelly

                                    i feel like
                                        i'm
                                    absolutely
                                      utterly
                              unconditionally
                                      insane.

the words of a madman   caitlin kelly

what a beautiful world we are in

(beauty is pain)

what a painful world we are in

chapter 2.
noyade.
drowning

the words of a madman　　　　　caitlin kelly

fake smile

sometimes smiles are
faked
so that the love
doesn't ache

sometimes my heart
cries
even when i act like
i'm fine

most times i love
even when there isn't
a dove

i'm broken
even when its not
spoken

the words of a madman　　　　caitlin kelly

~~i've written~~
~~so much~~
~~fucking~~
~~poetry~~
~~and there's~~
~~still nothing~~
~~i can do~~
~~about you~~
~~leaving~~
~~so i'll scream~~
~~my heart~~
~~and my soul~~
~~into these pages~~
~~i love so ever much.~~

~~and maybe i'll~~
~~publish it~~
~~so they can~~
~~read my~~
~~screaming mind~~
~~and all it's pain~~

~~and hopefully~~
~~someone will~~
~~whisper~~
"i understand"

- *just one person*

the words of a madman   caitlin kelly

i don't feel alive
i said
i feel like i'm dreaming
i said
help me
i said

except her mind never stopped
she stayed depersonalized
and acted like nothing was wrong
she would do anything to feel alive
during moments like this

the words of a madman   caitlin kelly

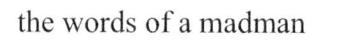

please stop romanticizing mental illnesses

the words of a madman   caitlin kelly

i'm walking
down the
street
back
to my car
yet i feel
a rush of panic
for no reason
at all
and i'm
dying on the
inside
gulping
for air
and all i was
doing was
walking to
my car
    - *anxiety*

the words of a madman   caitlin kelly

it's so weird how things can change so fast,
like you can meet someone and think they'll
be in your life a lot but the next second they
break you and someone else comes along
to pick up the pieces.

the words of a madman   caitlin kelly

i can't get rid of you
    i made you
i want you gone
    no, you want yourself gone
please go away
    i know you love me
i wish you never existed
    no. you shouldn't exist
you make me feel so worthless
    you are worthless

- a conversation with my depression

the words of a madman   caitlin kelly

forever
forever
forever
such an odd concept huh?
nothing lasts forever,
well nothing stays the same forever
everything grows up
everything decays
everything moves on.

the words of a madman   caitlin kelly

if you don't feel comfortable touching her purse
without permission
then you shouldn't feel comfortable
touching her body without permission
   - *no means no*

the words of a madman   caitlin kelly

i'm gonna run
into the streets
and scream

because that'll
make me feel
free

the words of a madman   caitlin kelly

an ode to depression

you brought me
countless of restless nights
just to remind me i'm losing this fight
this battle
this war
that you *dare* to conquer in my mind

you go by the name depression
and *oh god* how i've seen your
progression
in my mind
reminding me that all i want is to **die**

you're ruining my mind
yet the only words you'll allow me to say
is
"i'm fine"
"i'm fine"
"i'm fine"

"maybe happiness comes with your knife"
"maybe you should just end your life"
and as things get repeated over and over
they don't sound as bad when they were
first said,
i'm conditioned
to believe the words inside my head

you go by the name of depression
i'm always wondering how you have so
much strength
to become my obsession

the words of a madman — caitlin kelly

growing to unmeasurable lengths

and when i find someone to love
you won't let me test the shallow waters
of their heart
to slowly swim into the nice pool
instead you'll drag me in
by the ankle
to the rough freezing ocean
jumping to conclusions
showing me that drowning is better
then putting myself in pain again
that this one person is only there to pity
me
and that's what i should see
not to make me happy
because that would be too easy

you go by the name depression
and you never seem to want to leave
because your main goal is to see me
unhappy
because you tell me
"i don't deserve happiness"
"i'm not good enough"
and
"i'll never be"

when it's all said and done
i really do hope you had your fun

cause what a waste of time
would be your little trip to my mind.

the words of a madman caitlin kelly

you told me to find
my happiness

so i tried
to kill myself

cause maybe
i'll be happy then

the words of a madman   caitlin kelly

i don't deserve happiness

for some reason, when i get something
my depression doesn't think i deserve,
i get an urge. to pain myself.
to make it balance out.
that the happiness is something i don't deserve,
so i must feel pain.
i'm insane aren't i?

the words of a madman   caitlin kelly

brace yourself
for this wild ride
they call life

the words of a madman   caitlin kelly

i'm gonna stop telling
you when i'm hurt
cause i can tell
by your eyes
that you're sick
of throwing
pity parties
for me

the words of a madman   caitlin kelly

mouvements
7:05 pm

i'm just going through
the motions

i'm not even
living anymore

the words of a madman				caitlin kelly

why does it feel
like i'm constantly
sinking
further
and
further
under water
my heart is
beating out of my
chest
i can't breathe
i'm panicking
please save me
from drowning

- anxiety

the words of a madman   caitlin kelly

<u>*drowning*</u>
i feel like i'm drowning
but i can breathe
and everyone walks
above
like everything is fine
some even look at me
and act like they don't
see.

the words of a madman   caitlin kelly

i'll scream
and try to
get it out

but the only
problem
is screaming
won't make you
come back

as much as i
wish it would

screaming will
just make me
die a little more

knowing that
i'm like this
because
of you.

the words of a madman					caitlin kelly

entry:

I've always been an observer. If you go to a busy coffee shop and just watch people you can understand quite a bit about them. Everyone looks like they know exactly where they're going and what they're doing. I'm quite the opposite. I go with my gut. I do things when they happen. I'm someone that likes solitude but at the same time, I hate feeling lonely. I can be with ten people and still feel lonely. I can feel rejected or judged.
My dad always said you can tell a lot from a person's shoes. You can tell where they adventure or where they're going. I guess observing has helped me make my decisions based on people, even though they haven't been completely correct most times.
     I've always given people the benefit of the doubt though. I'm a very forgiving person. If you do me dirty and say sorry, 9/10 times I will forgive you. I've always been one of the people that feels bad. I will sympathize with you no matter what you do to me. That's one of the many things I would like to change about myself.

the words of a madman   caitlin kelly

are you okay?
       i'm okay

(i'll eventually be okay.. just not now)

                     solitude is your best friend
                           ... until it's 3 am

the words of a madman			caitlin kelly

as i studied psychology
i realized my thoughts are valid
that life after this
has no meaning
besides the journey
we choose to enjoy
and then we'll look
back on life together
and hopefully have
no regrets and a bunch
of stories to tell
    - *it comes with age*

the words of a madman   caitlin kelly

they told me i was holding up well
yet they didn't know the pain that i was holding
back

they said they were surprised i was ok
yet they didn't see the tears roll down my face at
the end of the day

the words of a madman

caitlin kelly

*what if hell
is the voices
and thoughts
in our heads?*

the words of a madman   caitlin kelly

we're prisoners of our own mind

the words of a madman   caitlin kelly

i also wish my anxiety wasn't existent

i get it's annoying to deal with
and i'm sorry,
i truly am
but if you want me you have to have my
anxiety too
because you can't pick pieces of me
to love
instead of loving the whole

the words of a madman   caitlin kelly

i woke up and looked into the mirror
and looked at the person in the reflection
and screamed
who are you
    - *depersonalization*

the words of a madman   caitlin kelly

*i don't want my decisions
based on if someone else
is watching me
and the life they gave me
to live*

    -   *from an atheist*

the words of a madman   caitlin kelly

i didn't lie
i just left out the
important details

the words of a madman   caitlin kelly

what they won't know

is that my heart will continue to flow

onto people worth my time

and that's not a fucking crime
- *the aftermath*

the words of a madman   caitlin kelly

I WANT TO SCREAM BUT
I CAN'T
BECAUSE THEY'LL
THINK SOMETHING
IS WRONG WITH ME
OR THEN
THEY'LL JUST FIND OUT
THAT THERE IS.

chapter 3.
perdu.
lost

the words of a madman   caitlin kelly

eleutheromania:
(n) the intense desire for freedom

the words of a madman   caitlin kelly

perdu.

*i'm lost
and
i don't know
how
to find
myself
yet
you claim
to know me
when i
don't even
know
myself*

the words of a madman   caitlin kelly

written by caitlin kelly
10-10-2017

Anxiety. I've lost so many people close to me because they don't understand it. They think I'm just being difficult. They think I'm fine. They think the panic in my head is fake. It doesn't help when they look at you oddly when you're panicking in your head. So they left me instead. That's okay because they didn't know what to do. I didn't need them anyways cause they weren't worth my time.

- *don't chase someone that walks away so easily*

the words of a madman			caitlin kelly

***i want to talk to you but my anxiety doesn't
want me to.***

the words of a madman   caitlin kelly

i constantly feel like a toy
used in multiple people's worlds

i'm there to help them
but if they don't need help
then they'll forget me

i'm not even living in my own world
anymore

i'm living in yours
and hers
and his…

the words of a madman   caitlin kelly

<u>nefelibata</u>
(n.) one who lives in the clouds of their own imagination

the words of a madman	caitlin kelly

peter pan
take my hand
way above the
clouds
to Neverland.

the words of a madman　　　　caitlin kelly

write how it feels..

*they told me to write how depression felt
my paper stayed blank
i couldn't describe it better*

*they then told me to write how anxiety felt
i couldn't find the right combination
of words to describe it
i couldn't describe it better than that.*

the words of a madman caitlin kelly

you asked me what was going on in my mind
i simply said "i don't know"

because if i told you what was going on
it would take me 20 years to explain
and by that time i'll realize
my thoughts are invalid
because i haven't been through
the worst times

- *"people have it worse"*

the words of a madman   caitlin kelly

i keep telling myself that
it's fine

i haven't had anything
traumatic happen in my
life

besides bullying and
heartbreaks

and getting beaten by
society

yet my life and family is
fine

but why do i still find myself crying at night

- *you said my life was fine*

the words of a madman						caitlin kelly

it was that moment
that i realized
no one will understand me
besides myself
and the only companion
i'll ever need
is myself
because that's the one
that will never leave

the words of a madman   caitlin kelly

~~runaway~~
~~to the castle~~
~~on the hill~~

~~because~~
~~maybe it will~~
~~fill the bucket~~
~~of the thing~~
~~we call our~~
~~dreams~~

~~and make~~
~~sure we aren't~~
~~seen~~

~~or else they'll~~
~~find out~~
~~that we aren't~~
~~conditioned~~
~~like the others~~
~~to believe in~~
~~false hope~~

the words of a madman   caitlin kelly

*tell me everything you want to change about me
cause i could write a whole book on what i hate
about myself*

the words of a madman　　　　　caitlin kelly

i
   dont
      want
         to
            live
              if
                 i'm
                    living
                       in
                          vain

the words of a madman   caitlin kelly

fuck
growing
up

the words of a madman   caitlin kelly

stop.

oh god caitlin,
stop falling
for them
so easily

you wonder why
you get so hurt
about it
in the end

the words of a madman   caitlin kelly

shredding.

i feel like i'm
shredding water
and it's fuckin'
tiring
and i didn't even
want to go
swimming
anyways

oh honey who broke you?

chapter 4.
cassé.
broken

the words of a madman caitlin kelly

broke me
february

alone
you left
you *broke* me
we weren't
the same.
is *anger*
in me
or did
i expect this?
you left me
you said nothing
you *broke* me.

the words of a madman   caitlin kelly

you told me i couldn't love you
if i didn't love myself

contrary
i love you more than
i could ever love myself

and that says something about you
and something about me

the words of a madman   caitlin kelly

love?
may

are we
in *love?*

or are
we merely
just happy
to find someone
like
ourselves?

the words of a madman　　　　　caitlin kelly

"you'll never find anyone else like me"

you make that sound like a bad thing

the words of a madman	caitlin kelly

10-13-2017

no amount
of therapy
can make
me forget
the pain
you've
put me
in.

the words of a madman caitlin kelly

my mind is so stuck
in the fucking past

and i can't let
the image of you
slip from
my mine

not even after
two years

the words of a madman caitlin kelly

someone asked
me
if i knew you

i froze up hearing
your name
and simply said

"i used to."

the words of a madman   caitlin kelly

after five months.
october

even after five months
    of leaving you

i am still scared of my own body
because of what you've done to it

you took advantage of my naive
                            innocent
                                      love for you

    and i'll never forgive you

because after i figured out that
you didn't even love me
my heart broke

and here i am trying to love
someone else with the broken pieces

i'll never learn will i?

the words of a madman   caitlin kelly

i've gotten over you
quite well
and quite quickly

because i came to the realization
that if you wanted to stay then
you would've

and i'm not going to change my way
to make you stay
and continue to lie
about who i am.

the words of a madman   caitlin kelly

i see your face like a heart attack

the words of a madman   caitlin kelly

as much as you say it's okay
i can't pull myself together
to believe your words

after all,
you did lie to me once before
when you said
"i love you"

emotional cheating.
march

cheating isn't just physical
it can be emotional
and that can hurt
so much more
than you could imagine

to see him smiling
brighter
larger
and bigger with a
girl that's not
you.

the words of a madman   caitlin kelly

11:47 am

you made it clear
that we're just friends

so let me stop embarrassing myself

and *please* stop talking to me.

the words of a madman caitlin kelly

"i love you"
was your
password
to get into
my pants
and force your
way in

"stop.. no"
was your
entry code
because you
couldn't figure
out what no means

because you
thought that
that's all i
wanted from you
not your attention
or your support
just your
fucking fingers
painfully
digging into
the only thing
left of me

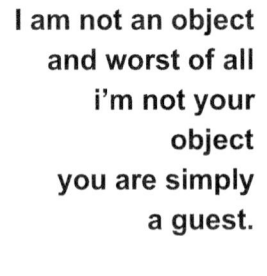

the words of a madman					caitlin kelly

**I am not an object
and worst of all
i'm not your
object
you are simply
a guest.**

the words of a madman   caitlin kelly

*idc who you are
if you love someone
you NEVER talk
shit about them
because love
is loving all their
imperfections
and not even having
anything bad
to say about
them.*

the words of a madman   caitlin kelly

<u>waiting</u>
<u>8:46 pm</u>

<u>the only problem with</u>
<u>waiting</u>
<u>is that they</u>
<u>may</u>
<u>change more</u>
<u>than you think</u>

the words of a madman   caitlin kelly

the memories of you
keep playing
over and over
in my head
and i'm not mad
because they're
my favorite story
the only reason why
i'm sad
is because
i miss the memories
and worst of all
i miss you

the words of a madman   caitlin kelly

11:49 pm
**what hurts
is when you're
right about
something you
wish you weren't**

- *you cheated.*

chapter 5.
coeur brisé.
broken heart

the words of a madman   caitlin kelly

you only
realize
how much
you miss
them
when
they're
gone.
        and you
        can't have
        them
        back.
                you lose
                track
                of time
                        until you
                        begin
                      to rhyme.

the words of a madman caitlin kelly

worst feeling
is when
the voice
in the
back of your
head
was
right.

the words of a madman		caitlin kelly

10:40 pm
who did you think you were
to tell me what i could
and couldn't do

the words of a madman   caitlin kelly

if he can walk away so easily then don't chase after him

if he can walk away so easily then don't chase after him

if he can walk away so easily then don't chase after him

if he can walk away so easily then don't chase after him.

    - *reminders*

the words of a madman   caitlin kelly

i heard your name spoken today
and for the first time
it didn't feel like a bullet in my gut
it didn't feel like a knife through my heart
and it didn't feel like the pain you meant to
leave me with

the words of a madman   caitlin kelly

i based my happiness
on you
and i knew it was true
though i denied it

the words of a madman   caitlin kelly

they told me to go home
then asked why i looked lost
because home was
your arms
and i don't know where
you went.

the words of a madman						caitlin kelly

it's absolutely insane how you can put so
much into someone and they can walk
away so easily

it will destroy you a couple times

but then you'll get used to it

that everyone you meet is now just a
phase in your existence

and the rest of your life will only rely
on yourself

the words of a madman   caitlin kelly

> don't think
> the one
> who broke you
> can fix
> you

the words of a madman   caitlin kelly

of course you didn't want to admit that you
fell for a fool *like him*

the words of a madman caitlin kelly

> you can't truly
> hate someone
> unless you
> once
> truly
> loved them.

the words of a madman   caitlin kelly

you can't break a glass
and expect a
"sorry"
to put it back
to the way
it was

the words of a madman   caitlin kelly

you fight for what
you
love
so obviously
to you this isn't
love
but why am
i still
fighting?

the words of a madman   caitlin kelly

fish in the sea

are there really
plenty of fish
in the sea?

because he
was the
only fish
that was
meant for
me.

the words of a madman caitlin kelly

**i never thought
a broken heart
could still
love**

the words of a madman   caitlin kelly

the light from the moon
makes her sing a tune
all about you

        her heart seems to have been completed
          even after the way she's been treated

your touch keeps her warm
almost like there was never a storm
in her years of life
where she used to cut with her knife.

the words of a madman　　　　　caitlin kelly

will you always?
october 2, 2017

will you always be here?
when my tears are fresh on my pillow
where i can't lay my head

when i call you up at 3 am
to hear your voice

will you always be here?
when the shadows of my head that tell me
to die come
holding a knife under my bed

will you always be here?
when i'm as happy as can be
when i'm no longer in sorrow
when i'm alive and well?

will you always be here?

the words of a madman · caitlin kelly

when i was with you.
9:09 pm

sparks flew
when i was with you.

butterflies flew
when i was with you

love i knew
when i was with you.

the words of a madman   caitlin kelly

i'm sorry
i can't give you all my heart
because it's shattered

and i need to keep some
pieces for myself

i'm not selfish
i swear

i'm just protecting
the remaining
pieces from
getting broken.

the words of a madman   caitlin kelly

you're not allowed to do that
you're not allowed to come into my life
and act like i'm your world

then leave like you
never even knew me

the words of a madman   caitlin kelly

you're just one big piece of bullshit

the words of a madman   caitlin kelly

*12:11 am
i hate myself
and i've
decided to
stop hiding
that from
your eyes*

the words of a madman   caitlin kelly

*your kind heart
is trying to protect mine
yet every time
you hold me back
it makes me want it more.
so i'll reach and reach
then you'll scold me
and i'll never learn
because sometimes
all i want to do is reach
and if i'm broken.
i want your
comfort
love
and arms wrapped around me
because that's all i need.*

*when i reached when you weren't looking
you didn't see i was hurt
because i didn't want to get scolded
so i acted like i was fine.
then all the anger and guilt built up inside
until i lashed out.
because you didn't notice the huge
scar on my arm
or maybe you did
you just didn't speak a word.*

-authoritarian parenting

the words of a madman   caitlin kelly

you had the ability to soar the sky
with your wings long before
he came and cut them
but you handed him the
scissors
hoping that he would be
the one to teach you to fly
instead he only wanted to
see you die
and fall to the ground
he may have cut your
gorgeous wings
but anything is possible
and your eyes
open up as he left
    -   for the better

11:02 pm
if you want to search for a new love
then look in the mirror
and love your heart out

the words of a madman   caitlin kelly

i've compared myself to all your female friends
and what i've noticed is
they're better than me in many ways
yet you tell me you only want me
which i find hard to believe

honestly if i were you
and i had a choice between me
or her
i would choose her too

- *that's how low i think of myself*

the words of a madman   caitlin kelly

when i'm talking
to you
it feels like
all my dreams came
true

the words of a madman   caitlin kelly

*we thought we
were on top of
the world.
but we were
just young
foolish teens
i hope you don't
forget me.*

the words of a madman   caitlin kelly

you can't walk away from
her
and expect her to wait for
your unlikely return

instead she'll run off
without you
and onto someone new.

the words of a madman   caitlin kelly

                              you never loved me
                              you just didn't want
                                   to be single
                            or you wanted attention
                           or i was good for your ego

                        you don't hurt the people you love

the words of a madman   caitlin kelly

feelings
change
i guess

the words of a madman   caitlin kelly

every single day
the thoughts of you
will get less
and less
and maybe i'll
finally get
over you

the words of a madman　　　　　caitlin kelly

*I keep promising
myself not to
fall for anyone
new but it's so
hard
just because
I met you.*

the words of a madman   caitlin kelly

the problem
with heartbreaks
is the fact
that not only has
the person hurt you as
you were so vulnerable

but the fact that
you lose yourself
just a little bit
and blame yourself
a little more

the words of a madman   caitlin kelly

*i'll act like my anxiety is nonexistent
this time so i don't have another
boy wishing away this burden
i live with everyday*

the words of a madman					caitlin kelly

*you only love me
when it's convenient for you*

the words of a madman   caitlin kelly

kissing is so weird
you're just pressing your
lips against someone
else's and for some reason
people think it's a disgusting
act of affection

the words of a madman   caitlin kelly

you thought the relationship was enchanted
but all he did
was take you for granted

the words of a madman　　　　caitlin kelly

when i realized i
started falling for you

i wept
because the pain from
last time came rushing
to my memories
and as much as i'll pray
you're different
i still won't be able to
give you my all
because i'm afraid to fall
again

the words of a madman   caitlin kelly

_ew_
cooties

chapter 6.
amour.
love

the words of a madman   caitlin kelly

ew
gross
love

the words of a madman   caitlin kelly

sunday
summer

coffee stains
bedsheets
our feet
touching
beneath
the covers
our hearts
connected
along
with the
others.

the words of a madman   caitlin kelly

you know you've fallen for someone,
when you stay up talking to them,
because talking to them is better
than all the dreams
you could possibly have sleeping

the words of a madman   caitlin kelly

i talked to the stars about you
and they believed everything would be true

the words of a madman   caitlin kelly

i'm not the one you want
because i'm not the one that's easy to fall
in love with

the words of a madman　　　　　caitlin kelly

*the poetry she
shares with you
will show you
her deep
intentions
her past
and
her heart.
don't take
her poetry
for granted.*

the words of a madman   caitlin kelly

i'm obviously too difficult to love
so don't waste your time lol

the words of a madman   caitlin kelly

a love letter to myself

the way her hair perfectly falls in front of her face
she's like a perfect storm
rough edges

oh and her eyes
her eyes are as beautiful as the ocean
you could stare into them all the time
so much to look into

she's been hurt so much
however still seems to wear that smile
that smile.. like she's never seen a bad day

she can look at anything with hope
her hopeful eyes are full of so much life
she just wants to live.

the words of a madman   caitlin kelly

primary colors of happiness:

red: hearts
building each other
holding each other
fixing each other

yellow: sunshine and daisies
you feel as if you're running
in a field of happiness
hand in hand

blue: the waves of the ocean
where you two
shared your first kiss
at the beach
on a saturday morning

the words of a madman											caitlin kelly

souls intertwined
love on my mind
happiness in laughter
could love happen any faster?

everyday words
turn into love songs
we're like love birds
that have no wrongs

the words of a madman   caitlin kelly

*i'm falling
for the
curve of your
smile i see
from
ear to ear*

*the light
in your
pupils*

*the way
your name
rolls off of
my tongue*

the words of a madman   caitlin kelly

*fingertips on
my ukulele*

*writing songs
about you
and me*

*singing adventures
of who we
used to be.*

the words of a madman   caitlin kelly

it's easy to tell
that i've fallen for
you
because i wouldn't
be singing
to the music in
the shower
in the best mood
after a day of
school

the words of a madman   caitlin kelly

your
smile
and
your
laugh
brings
me
peace

the words of a madman   caitlin kelly

                              foot on the gas
                           radio on full blast
                             singing along
                            to the new songs

                       this is what happiness is
                                      isn't it?

the words of a madman   caitlin kelly

a love poem for my best friend

dearest best friend,
how can you not see how beautiful your smile is,
when you laugh. how can you not see how pure
you are as you comfort me and my past. how can
you be so shy, as you are someone that everyone
should want as a friend.

dearest best friend.
you are a treasure, that i notice. others shall notice
too, but with time. and if
they don't notice your
beauty then, they weren't
good enough to see it
anyways. they aren't
worthy of your attention or
love.

dearest best friend,
you are the one that everyone needs in their life.
you are truly the most beautiful person inside and
out. you are one that can make a shit show into a
good old laugh and you are one of the only ones to
create teardrops from happiness.

dearest best friend,
you may not see it, but to me you are perfect.
you are beautiful
you are loved.
                    i love you.

the words of a madman   caitlin kelly

Everyday
    We talk
We laugh
    We smile
Everyday
    I fall in love
With you
    More and more
Over and over

the words of a madman   caitlin kelly

ways to say "i love you" without actually saying it.

text me when you get home
this made me think of you
i need you
i can't get enough of you
have fun
how did you sleep last night?
i'm proud of you
how was your day?
do you need help with that?
here let me get the door
take my jacket
i'm here for you
i miss you
drive safe
have you eaten today?
i brought you coffee
be careful
do you have your seatbelt on?

the words of a madman   caitlin kelly

moonlight.
june

moonlight on my skin
i have no more sins

i see you tomorrow
no longer in sorrow

i think i want to marry you
but you wouldn't have a clue

moonlight on my skin
tomorrow i'll see you again.

the words of a madman   caitlin kelly

we're only young
and dumb
but *god*
is it fun?

the words of a madman   caitlin kelly

perfection doesn't
exist
but i stopped
believing that
when i met
you
because all
your imperfections
are perfect
to me
and i know that
sounds
corny
and cliché
but i mean it

the words of a madman		caitlin kelly

i may be hella indecisive
but at least i knew right away that i liked you.

the words of a madman   caitlin kelly

it was two am
and he texted me

*the only people up at this time
are heartbroken or in love*

he asked me if i was okay today
if my breakdown recovered okay

*the only people up at this time
are heartbroken or in love*

i said yeah, i'm just hurt
i can't believe that happened

*the only people up at this time
are heartbroken or in love*

he comforted me
telling me about my whole life
that will proceed ahead of me

*the only people up at this time
are heartbroken or in love*

but this was the rare occasion where i was
heartbroken
but in love.

the words of a madman   caitlin kelly

head in the clouds

her heads in the clouds
as she's looking down
on the ground
for a boy that could be
worth her time

while the other boy in
the clouds is watching
her get let down
by the boys on the ground.

the words of a madman   caitlin kelly

be happy for no reason

because that way

the reason can never be taken from you

the words of a madman caitlin kelly

how can you love someone who can't find the power to love themselves?

things i've learned from heartbreak.

1.) *don't EVER say "i love you" if you don't mean it*

2.) *someone truly loves you if they take time out of their day and busy life for you*

3.) *the little things matter*

4.) *go with your gut*

5.) *anger reveals the truth*

6.) *don't ever stay with someone that puts you down and makes you change for them*

7.) *experiences are nice but if you actually see someone in your future then stay with them*

8.) *"pain is temporary" isn't true*

9.) *friends can break your heart*

10.) *mutual love is the best fucking thing in the world*

11.) *stop putting in effort for people who care less*

12.) *if they can walk away from you then LET THEM*

the words of a madman   caitlin kelly

i'm not a morning person
but you're the one that
makes me want
to wake up
each and every
morning

the words of a madman　　　　caitlin kelly

it was at that moment
that i realized
no one will understand me
besides myself
and the only companion
i'll ever need
is myself
because that's the one
that will never leave

the words of a madman			caitlin kelly

i gazed up at the
stars tonight

hoping you were
looking too

because maybe if we both look up at the same star

our wishes will become true

the words of a madman   caitlin kelly

maybe one day we'll cross paths back in LA

the words of a madman   caitlin kelly

hand holding mine
hearts intertwined

my mouth can't
form the three
special words

that can change everything.

the anxiety makes my heart beat
yet they're only
three
short
words.

i can't say it first

how would you react
what would i do then
what could i do then

if i say it too soon then
maybe my heart will get
stomped on
again
crushed
hurt
once again

oh god,
it's true though
why not state the truth

"i love you"

the words of a madman　　　　caitlin kelly

please fix yourself
before worrying
or trying to
fix me
-　love

the words of a madman   caitlin kelly

how the hell am i supposed to
define love
if it's a feeling
that's indescribable

the one that deserves you is the one that thinks they don't

the one that deserves you is the one that thinks they don't

the one that deserves you is the one that thinks they don't

the one that deserves you is the one that thinks they don't

the one that deserves you is the one that thinks they don't

the words of a madman   caitlin kelly

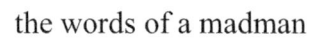

if life was a movie then you're the best part.

the words of a madman   caitlin kelly

i'm jealous of
anyone that
gets to
see you
everyday

the words of a madman					caitlin kelly

curled up
in my bed
with my cat
and my fluffy blanket
i'm trying to sleep
yet i can't get
you off my mind
and it's okay
cause i like
you on
my mind

chapter 7.
finalement.
finally

the words of a madman   caitlin kelly

you choose how your life is based on the choices you make

< insert happy ending here>

the end.

Printed in Great Britain
by Amazon